Sharks and Rays
of the Pacific Coast

AVA FERGUSON AND GREGOR CAILLIET

MONTEREY BAY AQUARIUM®

Monterey, California

The purpose of the Monterey Bay Aquarium is to stimulate interest, increase knowledge and promote stewardship of Monterey Bay and the world's ocean environment through innovative exhibits, public education and scientific research.

Acknowledgments This book draws heavily on the work of many researchers who kindly made their findings available to us, either directly or through the scientific press. We gratefully acknowledge their help. We would also like to thank Robert Lea, Linda Martin and David Powell for reviewing the manuscript and supplying us with valuable information and advice. Special thanks to Scott Martinek, too, for providing endless support during the writing stage.

Published in the United States by the Monterey Bay Aquarium Foundation, 886 Cannery Row, Monterey, CA 93940-1085.

Library of Congress Cataloging in Publication Data
Ferguson, Ava.
Sharks and rays of the Pacific Coast / Ava Ferguson and Gregor Cailliet

p. cm.—(Monterey Bay Aquarium natural history series)
At head of title: Monterey Bay Aquarium
ISBN 1-878244-02-7
1. Sharks—Pacific Coast (North America) 2. Rays (Fishes)—Pacific Coast (North America) I. Cailliet, Gregor M., 1943–
II. Monterey Bay Aquarium Foundation. III. Monterey Bay Aquarium. IV. Title. V. Series
QL638.9.F47 1990
597′.31′0979—dc20
90-5699
CIP

Photo and Illustration Credits:

Bancroft Library, UC Berkeley: 52 (bottom right)

Chastney, Rosemary/Ocean Images, Inc.: 19 (left)

Cailliet, Gregor M.: 11, 53

Caudle, Ann: 22 (bottom right), 27 (middle), (right), 28 (middle), (bottom), 30 (top), 34 (middle), (bottom), 36, 44

Faulkner, Douglas/Sally Faulkner Collection: 9 (bottom right)

Giddings, Al/Ocean Images, Inc.: 23

Hall, Howard: 4, 6 (bottom left), 8, 13, 15 (top right), 18 (middle), 22 (top right), (middle left, right), 24-25, 29 (top right), 30 (top right), 31, 38-39, 42 (top left), 45

Herrmann, Richard: 63 (top)

Kells, Valerie A.: 20 (bottom right)

Le Feuvre, Eric M.: 21

Matheson, Chip: 15 (lower right), 20 (top left), (middle right), 22 (top left), 51 (top)

Monterey Bay Aquarium: 2, 10, 41, 49, 55, 56, 57, 58, 59, 60 (top left), 61, 63 (bottom)

Moreno, Guillermo: 9 (middle)

Nakamura, Koji: 6 (bottom right)

Nicklin, Flip/Nicklin & Assoc.: 5, 15 (top left), 16 (top left), (top middle), (top right), 20 (middle left), 32, 42 (top right)

Princeton University Press: 9 (top)

Robison, Bruce: 47

Schafer, Kevin/Tom Stack & Associates: 40

Silberstein, Mark: 26

Snyderman, Marty: 7, 43, 51 (bottom)

Stafford-Deitsch, Jeremy from *Shark: A Photographer's Story*, Sierra Club Books: 29 (top left)

UCSC Special Collections: 52 (top right)

Wu, Norbert: 14, 16 (lower left), 17, 18 (top), 19 (top right), 20 (top right), 30 (bottom), 33, 34 (top), 35, 37, 60 (top right), 62

Series and Book Editor: Nora L. Deans
Designer: James Stockton, James Stockton & Associates
Printed in Singapore on recycled paper through Interprint, Petaluma, California

Contents

Flecks of sunlight glisten on the ocean's surface as a shark emerges from the dark waters below. Propelled by the sinuous strokes of its powerful tail, the shark glides easily through the water. Coal-black eyes contrast sharply with its cool gray skin.

Near the surface, the shark senses a change in the currents bathing its body. A slight turbulence emanates from the shimmering waters above. Without warning, the shark dives and disappears into the shadows, unseen by the swimmers overhead.

Swimmers in the cold, rich waters of the Pacific Ocean along the west coast of North America venture into the habitats of a great variety of sharks and rays. More than thirty-three kinds of sharks and their relatives spend time in Monterey Bay alone. Some live here year-round, in the shadowy kelp forests or dark deep sea. Others pass through on their journey along the coast as they roam the open sea.

Beautifully adapted to life in the sea, sharks mate, have young, feed, grow old and die in haunts far removed from our curious eyes. Only now, after centuries of study and pursuit, are we beginning to understand the life histories of these ancient fishes. Their stories make great reading, unfolding as they do, glimpse by fleeting glimpse.

1

SHARKS AND KIN

Sharks have long inspired our admiration and fear. For centuries we've sought to know more about these elusive fishes, gleaning only bits and pieces about their mysterious lives as we probe their often remote habitats. Today, as ways to observe wild and captive sharks improve, biologists are beginning to dispel long-held misconceptions about how sharks live and why they behave the way they do. In fact, studies reveal that sharks are not at all what we've commonly thought them to be.

Most sharks are harmless, timid creatures—more likely to flee from a swimmer than to attack. Few sharks actually live up to their reputation as man-killers. Some, like the white shark (*Carcharodon carcharias*), can and do attack people. But most sharks aren't as fierce as their reputations would lead you to believe. Only 67 of the more than 360 species of sharks are considered dangerous or potentially dangerous. Of these, only three species—the white shark, tiger shark (*Galeocerdo cuvier*) and bull shark (*Carcharhinus leucas*)—are regularly implicated in attacks on people.

The truth is that not all sharks are created equal; they come in a wide variety of shapes, sizes and dispositions. The blue shark (*Prionace glauca*), for instance, looks like your basic shark: it's long and slender with sharp teeth, strong jaws and a menacing grin. But the 50-foot whale shark (*Rhincodon typus*) resembles a baleen whale more than a shark, and feeds by sucking tiny plankton from the water. And not all sharks grow to immense proportions, either. When fully grown, the nine-inch-long pygmy shark (*Euprotomicrus bispinatus*) could easily fit in the palm of your hand.

Sharks swim throughout the world's oceans. Some species even venture into rivers and lakes. Bull sharks, for example, have been captured in the Mississippi River as far inland as Alton, Illinois, 1,750 miles from the sea! And while many sharks live near the surface, a few make their home in the deep sea.

The sleek blue shark, right, fits our typical image of a shark, but these fishes actually come in all shapes and sizes, ranging from the huge and harmless whale shark, left, to the tiny, young Japanese cat shark, below.

Sharks as a group defy generalizations. Some have very specific requirements and live only in a limited area. Other species thrive in waters worldwide. Some sharks travel in vast schools; others strike out alone.

Shark names are as varied as their habits and often suitably descriptive. Bizarre images come to mind when you hear names like angel shark, goblin shark, carpet shark, cow shark, saw shark, cat shark, hammerhead and wobbegong.

WHAT IS A SHARK? Sharks and their kin differ from other kinds of fishes in several ways. Sharks have no true bones; their cartilaginous skeletons are made entirely of the same tough, flexible tissue found in the tip of your nose.

Because they lack true bones, sharks belong to a separate class of fishes called Chondrichthyes, which means "cartilaginous fishes." This class includes skates and rays as well as more distant relatives, like ratfishes, or chimaeras, and elephant fish.

Shark skeletons are fortified with calcium phosphate and other minerals that strengthen their frames. Even so, there isn't much to a shark's skeleton: a skull, a spinal column, supports for the tail, median and paired fins and a few gill arches. So what holds a shark together? Mostly skin and muscle. That's why some sharks look so blubbery when they're caught and pulled from the water. Without the support of the surrounding sea, some sharks go limp and may actually be crushed to death by their own weight.

Much of the white shark's life history remains a mystery, due in part to its solitary habits and remote habitats.

SCALES   In the water, most sharks look smooth and streamlined, like many other fishes. But a shark's sleek appearance masks its rough exterior. Millions of tiny, toothlike scales called dermal denticles—literally "skin teeth"—cover its skin.

Like our own teeth, a shark's denticles have a central pulp canal surrounded by an outer layer of dentine capped with a layer of enamel. Under a microscope, these denticles look like thorns or prickly spines. The spines usually point backward toward the shark's tail. If you rub your hand along a shark's hide from nose to tail, its skin feels almost smooth. Run your hand the opposite way, against the spines, and it feels rough and abrasive, like coarse sandpaper. In some species, such as prickly sharks and basking sharks, the extremely sharp dermal denticles might cut or scrape your hand if you rubbed the shark the wrong way. In others, like smoothhound sharks, the dermal denticles lie flat and feel nearly smooth. Scientists often use these specialized denticles to distinguish one species from another.

You can judge a shark by its cover, or at least scientists can when looking through a scanning electron microscope. A fast-swimming blue shark's blunt denticles, top, reduce drag in the water, while those of the slower-swimming leopard shark, above, are more jagged.

ANCIENT SHARKS   Sharks belong to one of the most ancient groups of animals on earth. Most scientists think sharks evolved about 400 million years ago during the Devonian period—200 million years or so before the first dinosaurs appeared. The earliest known sharks were equipped much like modern sharks, with sharp, pointed teeth and cartilaginous skeletons, but their mouths were at the front of their heads rather than underneath. These early sharks eventually became extinct, replaced by other species. Scientists estimate that two to three thousand different species of prehistoric sharks once roamed the seas.

Most of our knowledge of ancient sharks comes from studying fossil shark teeth. Since sharks lack true bones, only their teeth become fossilized. However, imprints of entire shark skeletons are occasionally found. These rare finds reveal striking similarities between modern sharks and sharks that lived millions of years ago.

One of these ancient sharks, among the largest that ever lived, swam the seas about 60 million years ago. All we know of this monstrous shark, called *Carcharodon megalodon* (pronounced "car car uh don meg **gal** oh don"), is gleaned from its giant, fossilized triangular teeth. These fist-sized teeth range up to six inches long and look like those of a white shark. Scientists in the early part of the century estimated its length at over 100 feet with jaws measuring almost nine feet across, while today most biologists agree that *C. megalodon* was between 30 and 45 feet long. Early estimates were mistakenly based on inaccurate comparisons with the jaws and teeth of modern white sharks.

Because of their ancient lineage, sharks are often called "living fossils," which implies that sharks are primitive beasts, unchanged since life began. In reality, the sharks we know today arose long after the first bony fishes, and only a few living species of sharks are considered truly primitive. The majority of modern shark species evolved far more recently, becoming perfectly suited to life in the sea.

Complete fossils of sharks and rays, like this stingray, are uncommon.

RAYS AND SKATES Rays and skates may not look much like sharks, but they're closely related. Both are fishes and have skeletons of cartilage, not bone. But rays and skates belong to a separate group of cartilaginous fishes often simply called "rays." This diverse group includes sawfishes and stingrays; guitarfishes and electric rays; eagle rays and mantas—more than 400 different species of rays and skates in all.

Unlike most sharks, rays and skates are flattened. Broad, batlike fins attach directly to their heads, compared to the long, narrow fins extending out from a shark's body. And while sharks rely on their powerful tails to propel them through the water, rays and skates swim by flapping their pectoral fins like the wings of a bird. They use their long, thin tails for balance and steering, and in the case of stingrays, for defense.

What distinguishes skates from other rays? Skates generally have triangular or kite-shaped bodies with pointed snouts, tails bearing two dorsal fins and rough, spiny skin. Other rays have rounder bodies with broad snouts, and some possess long, whip-like tails that may or may not have a single dorsal fin. Rays generally have smooth skin, although there are exceptions. And while skates reproduce by laying eggs, other rays give birth to fully developed offspring—tiny rays that emerge alive and swimming.

Rays and skates range throughout the world's oceans, but are most common in tropical and temperate waters. Peaceful bottom-dwellers for the most part, they grub along the ocean floor, dining on hard-shelled clams and other invertebrates. A few species, like giant mantas (*Manta birostris*), swim at the ocean's surface, feasting on small fishes and plankton.

Flapping its broad fins, a bat ray glides through the water like a bird through air.

Rays, below, generally have rounder bodies while skates, bottom, are more triangular with pointed heads.

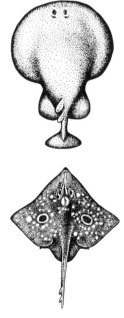

HOW DO YOU TELL A SHARK'S AGE?

You can't tell how old a shark is just by its size or appearance. Yet knowing a shark's age and how fast it grows is a vital step in discovering how long sharks live, at what age they reproduce and the length of their gestation period. Fisheries managers are especially eager for this information, since the age and rate at which a shark reproduces helps determine how many sharks can be caught without depleting the population. The dramatic increase in shark fisheries has encouraged research in this area, particularly at Moss Landing Marine Laboratories, where biologists are developing methods for determining the age and growth patterns of sharks and rays.

While determining a shark's age isn't easy, scientists can quickly calculate a bony fish's age by counting the pairs of calcified growth bands that develop on its bones and scales. Each band is often made up of many rings. Each pair of bands has one translucent (winter) band and one opaque (summer) band. Like the growth rings of a tree, each pair of bands often represents one year of life. However, the pair of growth bands don't always correspond to a single year, and band patterns vary among different sharks. What's more, some species of sharks lack these growth bands altogether.

Instead, scientists must rely on a variety of techniques for charting a shark's age and growth. One of the most common methods involves measuring and tagging wild sharks, then releasing them at sea. When a shark is recaptured, scientists compare the shark's total growth with the number of years it spent at sea, then calculate an average yearly growth rate to determine its age.

Researchers also inject tagged sharks with substances that cause the sharks' backbones to form distinctive growth bands. By counting these bands, scientists can estimate how long it takes for a shark to form a single pair of rings.

How fast do sharks grow? It varies, depending on the shark. Juvenile leopard sharks grow as much as four inches a year and have an average lifespan of about 25 years. Spiny dogfish, on the other hand, may grow only half as fast their first year, but may live for 80 years.

This section of a leopard shark vertebra has been stained with oxytetracycline to mark new growth. The bands outside the bright stains at the outer edges indicate new growth.

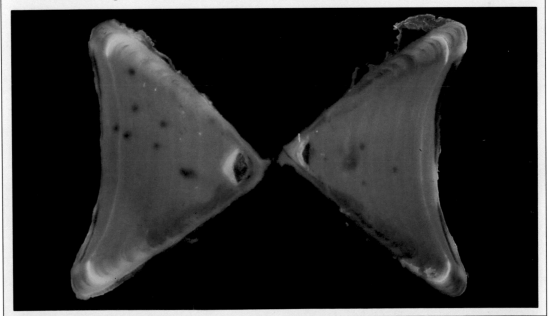

2

THE LIVES OF SHARKS AND RAYS

Sharks can be found worldwide—from the icy waters of the Arctic to the warm waters of the Great Barrier Reef. Most sharks live in tropical or temperate seas, while only a few survive near the poles. Where a shark lives depends on a number of factors, including water temperature and salinity, ocean currents, light, the kind of bottom surface, the presence of prey and, in a few cases, predators.

Many sharks can tolerate only the smallest temperature changes, so water temperature, for the most part, determines the global distribution of sharks. In temperate seas, where water temperature varies throughout the year, sharks like the thresher (*Alopias vulpinus*) make long seasonal journeys north or south to stay within their preferred range. Others, like the blue shark, are abundant in cool temperate waters, but also occur in the tropics, where they swim at greater depths in cooler water than at the surface. Pacific sleeper sharks (*Somniosus pacificus*) show a similar pattern but in different oceans. In the Arctic, sleeper sharks swim near the surface, while off California, they live primarily in the deep sea, where the water temperature more closely resembles Arctic sea surface temperatures.

MOVING THROUGH WATER Strong and graceful swimmers, most sharks cruise through the water like gliders, using their out-stretched pectoral fins as wings. Unlike the flexible pectoral fins of bony fishes that flap or fold back flat against their bodies, a shark's pectoral fins are stiff and rigid. On a straight glide, they provide lift and balance. In tight turns, these stiff fins help the shark steer. Triangular dorsal fins along a shark's back and the broad anal fin along its underside act like a keel on a boat and stabilize the shark, preventing it from rolling in the water.

When it comes to speed, open-ocean sharks are the fastest of all sharks. Muscular, streamlined bodies and powerful, crescent-shaped tails propel them at high speeds. Their curved pectoral fins are swept back like the wings of a plane to reduce drag and in-crease swimming efficiency. However, compared to swift-swimming fishes like tuna, most sharks swim slowly. They generally cruise at less than three miles per hour, although some, like makos, make short bursts of speed up to 30 miles per hour.

Bottom-dwelling sharks, by contrast, are generally sluggish swimmers. Their soft, round bodies possess small, feeble fins that provide little lift. Some bottom-dwellers actually crawl along the ocean floor on their pectoral fins.

A guitarfish looks like a cross between a shark and a ray as it glides along close to the bottom. While found considerably south of Monterey Bay, this banded guitarfish has similar habits to the guitarfishes common in the colder waters of Monterey Bay.

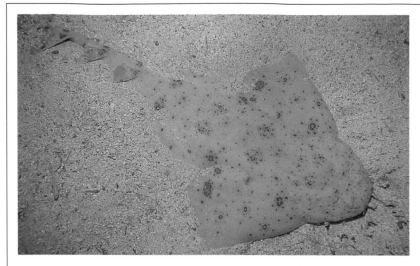

A half-buried angel shark blends in with the seafloor. While some sharks must constantly swim to keep water flowing over their gills so they can "breathe," others have muscles that pump water, allowing them to lie still.

A shark's body shape is closely related to its swimming style. Bottom-dwelling sharks swim like eels, undulating their entire bodies from tip to tail. Open-ocean sharks hold their bodies rigid and swim by flexing their powerful tails from side to side.

STAYING AFLOAT Sharks almost always swim, or lie peacefully on the ocean floor, but they rarely hover in midwater like other fishes. If a shark rests, it often sinks. Why? Their bodies are heavier than water, so they'll sink if they stop swimming. Most bony fishes, on the other hand, have the buoyancy-regulating organ called a swimbladder that helps them stay afloat. A fish's swimbladder works like an internal balloon. By adjusting the gases in this balloon, a fish becomes as light as the water around it and can hover at any level.

Since sharks have cartilaginous skeletons that are lighter than bony skeletons, they're more buoyant than you'd think. A shark also gets an added lift from its large liver filled with oils that are less dense than the surrounding sea. The oil in a shark's liver works like the gases in a fish's swimbladder—it floats in water and makes the shark slightly buoyant. The amount of oil in a shark's liver depends, in part, on how much food the shark eats. More food means more oil. The more oil a shark stores, the lighter it becomes in water. A buoyant liver gives a shark a real lift.

FINDING FRESH WATER If we lived in the ocean, our bodies would lose water and absorb salt. The result? Dehydration. Sharks and other marine fishes face the same problem and need a constant supply of fresh water to survive. Where do they get it? Most fishes get fresh water by drinking sea water and excreting the extra salt. But sharks use a slightly different approach.

In addition to drinking sea water, sharks retain urea and other metabolic wastes in their blood and body fluids—wastes that would normally be excreted. Their body fluids become as salty or saltier than the surrounding ocean, and their bodies absorb fresh water from the sea—just the opposite of what would happen to

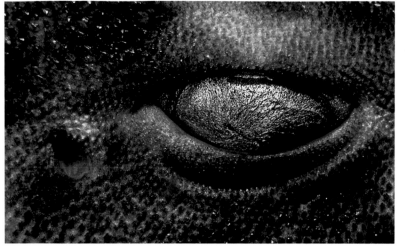

The swell shark eye, left, has a protective flap of skin. The narrow slit of an angel shark eye, top, watches for prey to ambush. The eyes of a ray, high up on its head, are sometimes all that's visible on the sandy seafloor, above.

you. For this to work, sharks must store waste products at levels that would poison most other animals. Researchers have yet to discover how sharks survive with such high levels of metabolic wastes in their bodies.

SENSING SURROUNDINGS Sharks rely on a variety of finely tuned senses, detecting sights, sounds and smells far more subtle than those we perceive on land. Biologists once thought sharks had poor eyesight, but we now know that certain sharks can see quite well, although some species appear to be farsighted. Sharks' eyes are far more sensitive to light than our own and they're especially quick at detecting moving objects. Sharks can also distinguish between certain shapes and sizes, and some species may be able to see different colors.

In murky ocean water, sharks probably rely less on their eyesight than on other senses. With their extremely keen sense of smell, sharks easily sniff out other fishes. When a shark detects a fish's scent in the water, it turns and swims upstream into the prevailing current, presumably toward the fish. Researchers have found that a number of different scents attract sharks, including the smell of blood. Studies on captive sharks show that some sharks detect blood in the water in concentrations as low as one part per 100 million—about the same as one drop of blood in a 1,300-gallon fish tank!

In addition to their keen sense of smell, sharks also possess excellent hearing. They're especially sensitive to irregular bursts or pulses of sound, including the low-frequency noises made by a struggling or wounded fish. Tape recordings of hooked fish may even cause captive sharks to bite and swallow loudspeakers placed in their tank. Some scientists think sharks use their ears more for coordination and balance than for hearing—much like we use our own internal ears.

In the ocean, sound waves are felt more than they're heard. Sound travels much farther in water than in air, and sharks can "feel" sound waves from over a mile away. Like many fishes, they

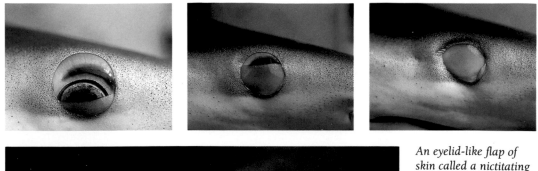

An eyelid-like flap of skin called a nictitating membrane, top, covers a blue shark's eyes to protect it from damage when feeding.

Sharks rely on their extremely keen sense of smell, excellent hearing and other special senses that detect vibrations in the water and minute electrical currents.

have a series of fluid-filled pores beneath their skin that forms a lateral line which senses vibrations in the water. (To find a shark's lateral line, look for a series of oddly shaped denticles with pores that run along the sides of the shark's body and around its head.)

In addition to sights, sounds and smells, sharks can also sense electrical currents in the water. Hundreds of tiny pores on the surface of their heads lead to sensory organs embedded in their skin. These sensory organs, called the ampullae of Lorenzini, detect minute electrical currents and minute changes in the direction of their intensity—as little as thirteen-billionths of a volt per inch! Sharks and rays have the greatest sensitivity to electrical currents of any animal. At close range, these predators sense the weak bioelectric fields produced by other animals—a kind of invisible electric aura that surrounds all living things, including people. Fine-tuned electroreceptors allow sharks to home in on bottom-dwelling fishes and other animals concealed in the sand.

Because of their sensitivity to electricity, sharks can also perceive the Earth's magnetic field. A shark's electroreceptors may work like an internal compass, helping the shark navigate over long distances. If so, this might explain how some sharks migrate over hundreds of miles of open sea and presumably return to the same feeding and breeding grounds each year.

Despite what we've learned about sharks in recent years, much about their sensory abilities remains sketchy. Among the mysteries surrounding shark senses are the tiny, cup-shaped pores, called pit organs, scattered over the surface of their skin. Under a microscope, these pores look like tiny taste buds. Researchers don't fully understand their function. Some think these pores may indeed be taste buds; others think they detect vibrations.

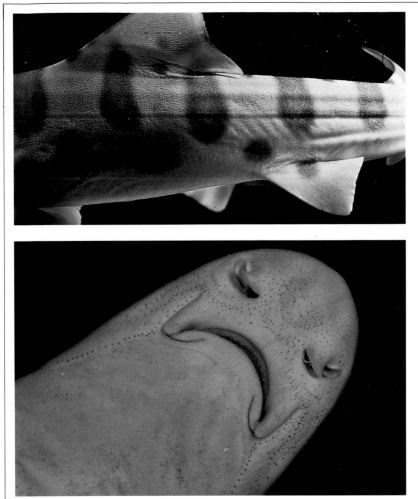

A shark, like other fishes, "feels" sound waves through a row of pores in its skin called a lateral line, barely visible along each side.

A shark's head is peppered with hundreds of tiny pores that help it detect the weak bio-electric fields of other animals.

FOOD AND FEEDING Sharks are often thought of as mindless eating machines—gulping down anything that swims. But, like people, sharks have shown distinct food preferences. Some species eat a single type of food almost exclusively. Blue sharks, for instance, feed extensively on fishes and squids, while horn sharks (*Heterodontus francisci*) favor spiny urchins and hard-shelled crabs.

Large sharks frequently dine on smaller sharks, including members of their own kind. Surprisingly, the largest sharks eat the smallest prey. The 50-foot whale shark sucks tons of tiny plankton and krill from the water.

The mouths of most sharks are on the underside of their snouts, but when feeding, these sharks don't have to turn sideways or roll over to bite their prey. They lift their snouts, thrust both jaws forward and extend their teeth outward, altering the entire shape of their heads. If the prey is too large to swallow whole, sharks often clamp their teeth into their victims, shake their heads with quick jerks, and tear out large hunks of flesh. The jaws of some sharks exert a tremendous force—up to 22 tons of pressure per square inch. That's about 300 times harder than people can bite. Sharks have even put holes in boats and bent propellers.

As a blue shark seizes a mackerel, above, its gill flaps are open as the shark draws water in through its mouth so it can suck in the fish.

Ink spurting from its mouth, this blue shark, left, feasts in a school of squid. The protective nictitating membrane half-covers its eye.

All sharks feed mainly on living prey, although a few, like the sleeper shark, will sometimes scavenge dead or dying animals. Despite rumors to the contrary, sharks don't actively seek out human flesh. Sharks are known to eat trash, however, if the tin cans and license plates in the stomachs of captured sharks are any indication. Tiger sharks are notorious for eating junk, including boots, beer bottles, raincoats, bicycle parts—even a chicken coop complete with feathers!

How much do sharks eat? It varies, depending on the species. Shortfin makos (*Isurus oxyrinchus*) hunt actively and may eat several times their weight in food each year. Others, like the deep-sea filetail cat shark (*Parmaturus xaniurus*) don't eat much at all. Sharks in captivity sometimes go for weeks and even months without eating, occasionally starving to death even when repeatedly offered food.

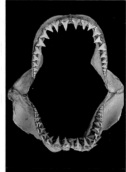

The jaws of a white shark, above, reveal sharply serrated triangular teeth well-suited to tearing chunks out of prey.

White sharks, left, inspire fear and dread, but these superbly adapted predators feed mainly on marine mammals like seals and sea lions.

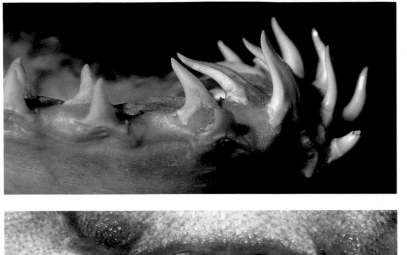

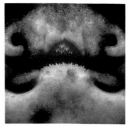

Shark teeth are as varied as shark diets. A mako, top left, seizes slippery fishes—the broken tooth in front will soon be replaced by the spare behind it. The cookie cutter, top right, takes small chunks out of larger fishes. The swell shark, above left, catches fishes and swallows them whole, while the horn shark, above right, crunches hard-shelled clams and crabs in its molarlike teeth.

SPARE TEETH Sharks are probably best known for their teeth—and for good reason. A shark's tooth is about as hard as steel and sharp enough to shave the hair from your arm. Unlike human teeth, a shark's teeth aren't anchored to its jaws and often fall out when the shark takes a bite. A large shark may use and lose many thousands of teeth in a lifetime.

Sharks have a lifetime supply of teeth and are constantly growing new rows of spares. A shark may have anywhere from 5 to 20 rows of spare teeth. Only the front row of teeth stick up; the others lie flat, like the shingles on a roof, one behind the other. When a front tooth breaks off, the one behind it moves forward. Young lemon sharks (*Negaprion brevirostris*) can replace an entire set of teeth in little more than a week.

A close look at a shark's teeth tells you about the kinds of food it eats. The narrow, pointed fangs of mako sharks help them grip slippery fishes. The broad, triangular, sharp-edged teeth of white sharks let them rip chunks out of seals and other large prey. Smoothhound sharks use their flat, pavementlike molars for grinding up hard-shelled crabs.

Sharks don't chew their food. After tearing, grasping or mashing their prey, they swallow the chunks whole. A white shark can swallow prey half its size. Two nearly intact six-foot sharks were found inside the stomach of a 15-foot white shark.

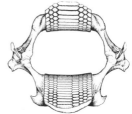

Bat rays grind their food with rows of cobblestonelike teeth.

HAVING YOUNG Sharks are especially unfishlike when it comes to producing young. Most fishes release clouds of eggs and sperm into the water and leave fertilization to occur at sea. But sharks rely on internal fertilization. Males have modified pelvic fins, called claspers, that transfer sperm directly into the females, much like a mammal uses a penis.

When sharks mate, the going can get rough. Females often bear scars from the males' "love bites."

While their breeding habits may be similar, sharks bear their young in dramatically different ways. Some sharks package their young in leathery egg cases, then abandon them at sea. Nourished by their yolk-filled egg sacs, the young sharks, called pups, develop on their own. After several months, one edge of the case comes apart and the tiny sharks emerge, alive and swimming.

Occasionally, egg cases wash up on beaches before the sharks inside can hatch. Beachcombers may know the pillow-shaped cases as "mermaid's purses." Swell shark egg cases come with strings attached—long, wiry tendrils at the corners that catch on

rocks and seaweed. These tendrils anchor the egg cases to the bottom and help prevent them from washing up on shore.

While some sharks cast their egg cases adrift, other mothers brood the developing embryos inside their bodies, then give birth to live offspring. Once they've depleted their yolk sacs, developing thresher shark pups actually feast on unfertilized eggs stored in their mother's oviducts. Unborn sand tiger sharks become cannibals and survive by devouring their smaller siblings.

Other sharks, like the blue shark, develop in much the same way as mammals. The young sharks absorb nutrients directly from the mother's bloodstream through umbilical cords attaching them to her womb. At birth, the young pups emerge as exact replicas of their parents, fully equipped for life in the sea.

Compared to bony fishes, many of which produce thousands of offspring each year, sharks bear relatively few young—usually less than a hundred, and in some species, only one or two. Also, most sharks have long "pregnancies," or gestation periods, lasting more than a year. Sharks also grow relatively slowly and take years to become sexually mature. These qualities make sharks extremely vulnerable to overfishing. Most shark fisheries have declined soon after they've begun, largely because the sharks could not reproduce fast enough to keep up with the demand.

A fully developed swell shark emerges from its egg case. Not all sharks and rays lay eggs; many actually give birth to live young. All skates, on the other hand, lay eggs, like the big skate egg case, below, packed with three eggs.

FOSSIL SHARK TEETH

Ten million years ago much of central California was covered by a vast inland sea. Ancient sharks roamed these shallow waters in great numbers, including the 45-foot-long *Carcharodon megalodon*—once the largest predatory shark on earth.

Over time, these sharks became extinct and disappeared, but their remains were buried in sediments on the ocean floor. Eventually, these sediments hardened into rock and were uplifted to form parts of the Santa Cruz Mountains which today overlook Monterey Bay.

Despite the dramatic change in the local landscape, evidence of ancient sharks and rays can still be found in these mountains, in the sand and gravel deposits once covered by the sea. Here, paleontologists have unearthed thousands of fossilized teeth, ranging from the tiny molars of a prehistoric bat ray to six-inch-long *C. megalodon* teeth—some of the largest ever discovered.

Shark teeth are among the most common marine vertebrate fossils. Why? Many sharks produce thousands of teeth in a lifetime. Extremely hard and resilient, these teeth become easily fossilized, like the bones of other animals.

The most common teeth found in the Santa Cruz Mountains are from two ancient species of mackerel sharks, close relatives of the shortfin mako also known locally as the bonito shark. Other teeth belong to an extinct species of tropical shark—a relative of the modern-day tiger shark. This finding suggests that millions of years ago the coastal waters of central California were warmer than they are today, and tropical species roamed this sea.

Fossil hunters have collected most of the shark teeth from road cuts and eroded stream beds, or from sand quarries located in Scotts Valley and Felton, north of Santa Cruz. Since the 1950s, sand and gravel from these quarries have been used to pave roads throughout the Monterey Bay area, leaving the sidewalks of some downtown cities literally lined with shark teeth.

A fossil tooth of the extinct Carcharodon megalodon, *found in the Santa Cruz mountains.*

3

HABITATS OF SHARKS AND RAYS

The rich waters off the Pacific coast harbor an amazing variety of cartilaginous fishes. In Monterey Bay in particular, at least 33 different species pass through or find permanent refuge—a remarkable number given the bay's relatively small size. Some species reside here year-round. The rest visit when conditions are right, departing with a change in seasons, or when a favorite food becomes scarce, or for reasons we have yet to discover.

Why do so many species call the bay home? The interplay of cool waters, geographic location, marked seasonal changes and wealth of habitats results in the diverse mix of sharks and rays.

The Pacific Ocean off the coast of California actually falls within two marine regions: a cool-water region extending north from Pt. Conception to southeast Alaska, and a warm-water region stretching south, almost to the tip of Baja California. The water in Monterey Bay is noticeably cool, averaging 55°F compared to 63°F coastal waters farther south.

Water temperatures dictate where certain species of sharks and other cartilaginous fishes live. Acutely sensitive to the temperature ranges along the coast, these fishes occupy habitats most suited to their needs. Many of the sharks and rays in Monterey Bay are cool-water species, and while they may be found up and down the coast from Baja California to British Columbia, most are more common north of Pt. Conception. Surprisingly, the species found permanently in the bay more closely resemble those you'd find off British Columbia—over 1,000 miles north—than the populations off Santa Barbara, only 250 miles south.

Despite the cooler water temperatures in central California, southern species occasionally venture up the coast and settle in. Warm-water migrants appearing in Monterey Bay may include thornbacks (*Platyrhinoidis triseriata*), shovelnose guitarfish (*Rhinobatos productus*), horn sharks, swell sharks (*Cephaloscyllium ventriosum*) and round stingrays (*Urolophus halleri*). Abundant off southern and Baja California, these fishes are rarely seen north of Pt. Conception, and only a small number survive in the bay. Scientists doubt if warm-water species are able to reproduce in such cool water. Their presence in the bay is probably maintained by recruits from southern California.

Why do these sharks and rays swim or wander up the coast? No one knows for sure. Some scientists think fishes travel north during periodic occurrences of El Niño—a cessation of winds and a shift in ocean currents along the equator that increases the temperature

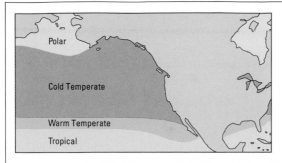

The cool water along the Pacific coast becomes warmer farther south, which greatly affects where you'll find certain species.

Blue sharks, like this explorer, are not commonly seen in kelp forests during the day.

of surface waters farther north. Previous El Niños extended the ranges of many marine fishes, including sharks.

In 1983, for instance, when an El Niño warmed the waters off the Pacific coast, fishermen in southern California caught hundreds of pelagic thresher sharks (*Alopias pelagicus*). Previously recorded south of San Diego, during El Niño they were caught as far north as Pt. Conception. A year later, an oceanic whitetip (*Carcharhinus longimanus*) was caught near Santa Catalina Island, off southern California. This shark usually lives in the tropics, but with the shift in warm waters, its range extended hundreds of miles.

Time of year greatly affects which shark species you'll find in the bay. Just as on land, coastal waters off central California experience distinct seasons, marked by changes in water temperature. During spring and summer, northwesterly winds blowing down the coast combine with the Earth's rotation to push surface waters offshore. Colder water wells up to take its place, giving Monterey Bay its lowest temperatures of the year.

During fall (from August to October), the prevailing winds die down and cease to draw cool water from below. Warm oceanic water from far offshore drifts into the bay, raising water temperatures. Along with this warm-water mass swim large open-ocean sharks, such as shortfin makos and blues. These seagoing sharks may linger in the bay for a month or two.

Few other places in the world match the richness and diversity of the Pacific coast's Monterey Bay. Its waters encompass a wide variety of habitats—from the shadowy realm of the kelp forest to the sunlit surface of the open sea—providing a wealth of living spaces for sharks and rays. Many of these habitats are found throughout the world's oceans. Others, like the wetlands of Elkhorn Slough or the depths of Monterey Canyon, are rare even along the California coast.

SLOUGHS AND ESTUARIES Narrow winding waterways edged with marshy plants and muddy ground, sloughs are wetlands inundated with fresh water or salt water. Sloughs provide shelter and food for sharks and rays, some of which give birth in the slough's shallow waters. Although they're becoming rare along the coast of California, some significant wetlands are located midway between Monterey and Santa Cruz, where Monterey Bay's waters turn away from the sea and flow inland at Moss Landing. The pounding waves of the outer shore give way to a quiet inlet known as Elkhorn Slough. This narrow waterway winds back from the coast like a river, stretching nearly seven miles inland. Along the way, the slough's main channel, used as a seaway by pleasure boaters, branches into a sinuous maze of tidal creeks—shallow tributaries that extend the slough's expanse over four square miles of marsh.

This shallow backwater might seem like an unusual place to find sharks and rays. But the slough is more than a series of channels filled with sea water. Saltmarshes and mud flats of incredible richness border its banks. Like other wetlands along the Pacific coast, these wetlands teem with fishes, shellfish and other invertebrates, which, in turn, provide an important source of food

Shallow slough waters offer refuge and food to several species of sharks and rays.

for sharks and rays. The slough's placid waters also provide shelter, offering hideouts from larger sharks in the deeper waters offshore.

The waters of Elkhorn Slough rise and fall twice each day with the flow and ebb of the tides. During high tide, water from the main channel sweeps over the shallow banks, flooding the neighboring marshes and mud flats. As the water rises, leopard sharks (*Triakis semifasciata*) spread out over the flats in search of food. Boldly patterned, these sharks are easily identified by the distinctive black spots that give them their name.

Young leopard sharks in the slough feed mainly on small crabs that skitter along the surface of the mud flats. As they grow

Leopard shark

older, the sharks graduate to other prey—larger crabs, worms, fishes and even other sharks. As they cruise along the flats, adults occasionally nip off clam siphons or suck up worms from the mud, then retreat to the main channel as the tide waters recede.

Bat rays (*Myliobatis californica*) have also adjusted to this tidal rhythm. At high tide, these sleek rays emerge from the slough's main channel to seek out richer hunting grounds. Gliding over the submerged mud flats, bat rays flap their large pectoral fins like wings. They also dig up food with their wings, flapping them against the bottom to unearth clams and worms buried beneath the silt and mud. Walk along the mud flats at low tide and you may see long, deep trenches etched in the mud—a sure sign that bat rays have been feeding. Females may grow up to six feet across; males have slightly smaller wingspans.

Bat ray

Why are they called bat rays? No one's quite sure. Some say it's because of their batlike flight, others claim it's because of their large, batlike heads. Their scientific name, *Myliobatis californica*, which means "California grinder ray," refers to the way they eat. Bat rays have flattened teeth—like cobblestones—used for grinding instead of tearing their food.

Many of the sharks and rays that frequent Elkhorn Slough appear to follow a yearly cycle—moving into the slough during spring and summer, then departing for offshore waters in winter. The slough serves as a seasonal nursery ground for a number of fishes, including leopard sharks and bat rays. Both species give birth in the slough, and scientists suspect that a few other sharks and rays may breed here as well.

The slough's tidal creeks are especially busy during spring, when leopard sharks come in to bear their young. Mother sharks give birth between April and June, sometimes bearing as many as 29 pups in one litter. Young leopard sharks appear to stay in the slough for several months. Scientists suspect that some remain year-round, while others reside offshore, perhaps returning to feed and give birth.

Bat rays, too, are year-round residents. They're most common during spring and summer, when females move in to breed and give birth. A female bat ray may give birth to a half-dozen off-spring in a single litter. The shiny newborn rays emerge tail first, their soft, leathery wings wrapped around their bodies. To protect the mother during birth, the newborn's stinging spine is rubbery and covered with a sheath. It soon hardens, though, ready for defense within a few days.

Why is the slough such a good place to grow up? Scientists aren't absolutely sure, but they suspect the slough provides juveniles with plenty of food while offering them safety from larger predators offshore. The slough's murky waters may also conceal juveniles from predators in the slough, including adult leopard sharks.

Other sharks and rays spend part of their lives in the slough, although we're not quite sure why. In the fall and winter, some round stingrays swim from sand flats just offshore to hang out in the slough's main channel. Catch records from shark derbies held during the 1950s, as well as more recent studies, show that nearly all the stingrays caught in Elkhorn Slough were adult males. Studies from southern California show a similar pattern: male stingrays are found almost exclusively in shallow, nearshore waters, while females stay in deeper, offshore waters.

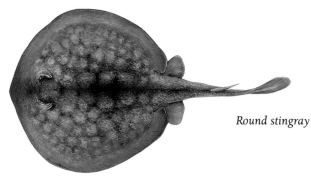

Round stingray

The onset of winter in the slough also marks the arrival of gray smoothhounds (*Mustelus californicus*). These diminutive sharks move into shallow water during November and December, occasionally followed by their close relatives, the brown smooth-hounds (*Mustelus henlei*). Why these sharks visit the slough is still a mystery; like stingrays, neither one breeds there. Perhaps they're coming in to feed. Most stingrays and smoothhounds depart by early summer, when the cycle in the slough begins again.

Gray smoothhound

Kelp forests, above, provide a wealth of habitats for sea life, from schooling fishes to leopard sharks, like this pup seeking shelter on the kelp forest floor.

KELP FORESTS Beyond the crash of pounding surf, tall stands of seaweed called giant kelp (*Macrocystis pyrifera*) rise up from rocky reefs along the Pacific coast and in Monterey Bay. From shore, these groves of waving kelp look like brown mats floating on the water's surface. But beneath this dense tangle of blades lies a lush undersea forest. Here, schools of surfperch dart beneath the tree-like canopy of kelp. Turban snails and kelp crabs roam among the fronds, while brightly colored sponges and anemones carpet the rocks below.

Along the bottom, leopard sharks lurk in the shadows. In the kelp forest, these active, fast-swimming sharks feast on anchovies and other schooling fishes. Darting through schools with their mouths wide open, they snap up fishes along the way. Divers in Monterey Bay report that groups of leopard sharks sometimes congregate in the kelp forests during winter, then mysteriously disperse. Some may move into Elkhorn Slough to breed, while others may hide out in the kelp beds or swim farther offshore.

Angel shark

Unlike leopard sharks, most kelp forest sharks are slow-swimming sluggish creatures that spend their lives on the ocean floor. Pacific angel sharks (*Squatina californica*), for instance, nestle in sandy channels along the fringes of the forest. Often confused with rays, they're round and flat and have broad pectoral fins shaped like angel wings—the source of their name.

An angel shark lies hidden in the sand, waiting for an unsuspecting fish to swim within range.

Although rare in Monterey Bay, angel sharks are common in southern California, where they're often seen resting in the sand. Despite their sedentary appearance, these predators lie in ambush along the bottom, waiting for small fishes to swim within striking range. When an unsuspecting fish passes overhead, the angel shark lunges upward, sucks up the fish in its huge mouth, then swallows it whole. Divers who disturb a resting angel shark are often surprised by the shark's ferocity. If provoked, this normally peaceful shark may snap and bite, inflicting a painful wound.

Like the angel shark, the Pacific electric ray (*Torpedo californica*) buries itself in the sand, leaving only its dark eyes exposed. For years, researchers thought these rays rarely moved. But recent studies reveal that electric rays are actually nocturnal, swimming

Pacific electric rays generate enough power to stun other fishes and shock unwary divers.

over rocky reefs at night in search of fishes and other food.

Though soft-bodied and slow-moving, the electric ray is a formidable predator. When a fish swims by, the electric ray pounces on it and delivers a stunning jolt. Electric organs embedded on either side of the ray's head generate a spinetingling current that can zap prey—and sometimes shock predators and human divers. In large rays, the electric organs produce a current of up to 80 volts—about the same voltage as ordinary household current. Researchers studying electric rays in Santa Barbara found they could even get the rays to light up flashcubes under water. An electric ray's energy sources are limited, however. It uses up most of its shocking power on the first jolt and must rest and recharge after each attack.

Down on the reefs, horn sharks hide out in the shadows. Like many creatures of the kelp forest, these sharks are beautifully masked with the surrounding colors of the community—mottled greens and muddy browns. Camouflage helps them elude larger sharks and other predators.

Timid animals, horn sharks spend most of the day holed up in dark crevices or caves, emerging at night to feed on clams and shellfish. True bottom-dwellers, horn sharks swim poorly and sometimes crawl along the rocks on their pectoral fins. Their soft, lumpy bodies, flabby fins and gnarled, piglike snouts contrast sharply with the sleek profiles of open-ocean sharks. High bony arches above their eyes give horn sharks perpetually furrowed brows and one of their many nicknames, "bullhead shark." Other nicknames include "pig shark" because of their unusual snouts, while the common name—horn shark—stems from the sharp hornlike spine located in front of each dorsal fin. The scientific name, *Heterodontus*, means "different teeth," referring to the two different kinds of teeth lining their powerful jaws—flat, grinding molars in the back and sharp, biting teeth in front.

The horn shark is named for the sharp, hornlike spine on its dorsal fins, below left. The spiral flanges on a horn shark egg case make it difficult to get out of tight crevices.

Though rare in Monterey Bay, horn sharks occasionally share the rocky floor with swell sharks, another uncommon species in the bay. Like the horn shark, the swell shark is camouflaged. Mottled colors help it blend in with the rocks, concealing it from larger sharks above. If discovered, the swell shark gulps water and swells up like an inflated balloon. Instead of floating away, the shark wedges itself more firmly between the rocks. Wedged in tight, a bloated swell shark can be difficult for predators to dislodge, let alone swallow.

You'll often see swell sharks lying on top of each other, or piled up like logs.

Surprisingly, this slow-swimming shark dines on fast-swimming fishes. Like the horn shark, it feeds primarily at night when many other fishes are resting. Rather than swim in pursuit of its prey, the swell shark lies patiently on the bottom, lunging at unsuspecting fishes as they swim by. Or it might sit on the bottom and "yawn," slowly opening its mouth until a careless fish—apparently mistaking the shark's mouth for a crevice—unwarily swims inside. Snapping its jaws shut, the swell shark traps its prey and swallows it whole.

SANDY SEAFLOOR Most of Monterey Bay is surrounded by long stretches of sandy beach. Beyond the shoreline, these beaches slope gently seaward until they blend with the bay's deeper muddy floor. At first glance, this shallow plain seems lifeless and barren, like an undersea desert. But life abounds on the sandy seafloor. Hordes of clams, anemones, worms, crustaceans and other invertebrates burrow into the sand and mud, while fishes swarm in the shallows. This rich bounty attracts bottom-dwelling sharks, skates and rays as well as sharks that cruise through the waters overhead.

Near shore, strong waves sweep over the sand, unsettling everything. Because of the constant surge, animals here must keep a low profile, lying along the bottom or burrowing beneath the coarse sand. The thornback holds its ground against the churning surf by digging in, leaving only its back exposed. To breathe, the ray inhales water through two small holes, called spiracles, on top of its head and exhales through its gills underneath. This prevents the ray from breathing in sand and silt, which could damage its sensitive gills.

The thornback gets its name from the rows of sharp, thornlike denticles that line its back. Its thorny armor discourages sharks and other predators from attacking the otherwise defenseless ray. Most of the time, though, the thornback merely stays out of sight. Like many animals of the sandy seafloor, the camouflaged thornback's dappled back blends perfectly with the sand, concealing it from predators overhead.

Like thornbacks, round stingrays spend most of their time lying quietly on the bottom, half-buried in sand and silt. If disturbed or stepped on, the ray may whip its tail and lash out with a sharp, daggerlike spine.

A stingray's spine isn't at the tip of the tail, as most people think. Instead, it lies on top, a third of the way down, closer to the base. Glands along the sides of the spine produce a paralyzing venom. In people, stingray venom affects the heart and nervous system, causing nausea and slight paralysis. Although painful, a stingray wound rarely proves fatal.

Unfortunately, beachgoers often don't see the stingray until it's too late and may accidentally step on a ray when they enter the

A thornback burrows in the sand, relying on camouflage for survival. Three rows of sharp "thorns" along its back help to discourage would-be predators.

A stingray's spine lies partway up the tail, not at the tip as is commonly believed.

water. The best way to avoid a stingray's spine is to practice the "stingray shuffle." As you enter the surf, slide your feet along the bottom to stir up the sand and scare off any stingrays resting on the bottom. A stingray's best defense is flight, and given half a chance, it will quickly swim out of the way.

One of the strangest-looking creatures found along the sandy seafloor is the shovelnose guitarfish—named for its pointed snout and guitar-shaped body. Although this odd-looking fish resembles a shark, it's actually a ray. Scientists consider guitarfishes to be among the most primitive of all living rays and have traced their origins back more than 100 million years.

Shovelnose guitarfish

Big skate

Like most rays, guitarfishes are attuned to life on the bottom and spend most of their time lounging in the sand or cruising just above the seafloor. But while most rays swim by flapping their large pectoral fins, guitarfishes rely mainly on their sharklike tails to propel them through the water.

Although guitarfishes may look and swim like sharks, their teeth are small and blunt, like those of other rays. Guitarfishes eat hard-shelled invertebrates, including clams and crabs, and an occasional fish. Swimming with their shovel-like snouts close to the ocean floor, guitarfishes search for meals on the seafloor.

Farther offshore, the restless surf nearly ceases. Waves stream gently over the bottom, depositing layers of fine silt and mud. Skates burrow into the muddy ooze, munching on shrimps, worms and clams. The largest skate in the bay is the big skate (*Raja binoculata*), which may grow to be nearly eight feet long and weigh up to 200 pounds. Flat and kite-shaped, the big skate covers itself with sand and mud until only its dark, bulbous eyes protrude. Its grayish, mottled body blends in with the bottom, helping to conceal it from sharks and other predators—but only if the skate stays still. Once detected, a skate darts up from the bottom and swims away, rippling its fins like a magic carpet.

Guitarfish sweep the sandy seafloor for crabs and other hard-shelled invertebrates.

Two large, black spots on the big skate's fins look like eyes. Some scientists suspect these "eyespots" may fool potential predators. Instead of lunging for the skate's sensitive eyes, an attacker that mistakenly lunges for the eyespots ends up with only a bit of the fin or a piece of the tail, while the skate speeds safely away. Eyespots may also make a small skate appear larger, causing a predator to seek other prey altogether.

In Monterey Bay, skates are fished exclusively for their "wings," which are sold in fish markets and restaurants throughout the state. Skate wings have the flavor, texture and color of scallops, and plugs cut from the wings are sometimes substituted for the more expensive mollusc. However, experienced seafood consumers can easily tell the difference. In scallops, the "grain" of the flesh runs vertically, while in skates, the "grain" runs horizontally.

According to the California Department of Fish and Game, 25,000 to 50,000 pounds of skate wings are landed in Monterey Bay each year, a figure that represents only a fraction of the skates actually caught. While skate wings are considered a delicacy in Europe, most Americans turn up their noses at the thought of eating skate. This makes it difficult for fishermen here to sell their catch. Instead, the majority of skates caught off the coast of California are thrown overboard and never reach consumers' tables.

In the waters above the sandy seafloor, sharks dominate the scene. Here, the sevengill shark (*Notorynchus cepedianus*) hunts for crabs and fishes, including skates and rays hidden along the bottom. Sometimes called cow sharks, sevengills have flattened heads and stout, round bodies. Off northern California, these sharks are commonly caught near shore and in Humboldt Bay and San Francisco Bay during spring and summer. They are only rarely spotted in Monterey Bay.

Sevengill

Spiny dogfish

Several unusual features distinguish sevengills from other sharks, including a single dorsal fin, a poorly calcified skeleton, and seven gill slits instead of the usual five. These characteristics prompted scientists to consider sevengills—along with their close relatives, the sixgills (*Hexanchus griseus*)—among the most primitive of sharks. Sevengills appear to have changed very little over the last 100 million years.

One of the most abundant sharks in the bay lives just above the sandy seafloor. Here, spiny dogfish (*Squalus acanthias*) often swarm in dense schools numbering in the hundreds. As its name implies, the spiny dogfish sports a sharp, venomous spine in front of each dorsal fin. Among the smallest sharks in Monterey Bay, this shiny, slate-gray shark rarely grows over four feet long.

Despite their diminutive size, spiny dogfish can be extremely aggressive and are known for relentlessly pursuing their prey. The name "dogfish" stems from their habit of feeding in packs. They'll eat almost anything they can get their strong jaws and teeth on, including squid, fishes, crabs and shrimp. Newborn dogfish will attack fishes two to three times their size.

A creature of habit more than habitat, the spiny dogfish ranges widely over the bay, from the sunlit shallow waters near shore to the inky depths of the submarine canyon. Spiny dogfish also travel long distances. A tagged shark released from Washington state showed up eight years later off the coast of Japan, more than 5,000 miles away.

Schools of spiny dogfish often split up according to size and sex, though young sharks—both male and female—tend to stick together. In spring, large groups of adult females migrate toward shallow water where they give birth to their young. Like most sharks, spiny dogfish grow slowly. Females usually don't reproduce until they're at least 20 years old. Dogfish embryos take two years to develop, longer than whales or elephants. Although slow to mature, spiny dogfish may live to be over 80 years old.

Spiny dogfish were once fished in great numbers in Monterey Bay. During the 1930s and '40s, these sharks were valued for their liver oil, which contains large amounts of vitamin A. Today, most fishermen in the bay consider spiny dogfish a nuisance. The sharks are notorious for tearing through fishing nets and stealing the fish inside. When tangled in a net, dogfish can be extremely difficult to remove. Their sharp teeth and venomous spines make them hazardous to handle.

A spiny dogfish tangled in a gill net.

Much of what we know about the biology of sharks in general comes from studying the spiny dogfish. Each year thousands of these sharks are preserved as specimens and dissected in high school and college biology classes around the country. Most studies of dogfish have focused on the shark's anatomy and physiology, leaving a lot of questions unanswered about their habits in the wild.

OPEN OCEAN Beyond the continental shelf, the shallow coastal waters give way to a broad expanse of open sea. Here, large seafaring sharks patrol the upper waters in search of fishes and other prey. The most famous of these is the white shark. Few creatures on earth inspire as much fear and dread. Though rarely spotted in Monterey Bay, the white shark is feared for its random attacks on surfers and divers in the area. Despite its reputation, this shark averages just one attack a year off the entire coast of California.

The white shark is what most of us think of when we hear the word "shark"—a large, toothy predator able to kill or inflict terrible wounds on people. No other shark is surrounded by as many myths and stories. Surprisingly, we know very little about the life history of white sharks—where they breed, how long they live, or even why they attack people. Their solitary habits and remote habitat make it difficult for scientists to gather detailed information about them.

Researchers have managed to piece together a few basic facts about this shark's life. Despite accounts of white sharks reaching 30 to 45 feet in length, catch records suggest that most grow no longer than 20 feet. The largest white shark on record—a female caught off western Australia in 1984—measured 19½ feet.

While few white sharks have been observed for long periods in the wild, biologists believe these sleek ocean predators spend most of their time cruising the open sea. White sharks generally swim slowly, although they're capable of great bursts of speed. A white shark tagged with a radio transmitter off Long Island, New York, covered 115 miles in a little over two days, giving it an average speed of only two miles per hour. The majority of whites swim in cool temperate seas and are most often seen traveling alone or in pairs.

Much of what we do know about white sharks has come from sightings off central California. The relative abundance of white sharks in these waters has led divers to call this region the "white triangle." It covers a thousand-square-mile area stretching from

Año Nuevo Island north to Tomales Bay and extending offshore to the Farallon Islands, west of San Francisco. Over half of all the recorded white shark attacks in California occurred in these waters. Because of the bloodiness of the attacks, local media now refer to the area as the "red triangle."

Since 1970, researchers from the Point Reyes Bird Observatory and other institutions have been studying white sharks off the Farallones. The sharks are attracted to seal and sea lion colonies, particularly the large elephant seal colonies at Año Nuevo and South Farallon islands.

White sharks off the Farallones seem to follow a seasonal pattern of abundance based on the seals' breeding cycles. During spring and summer, the sharks are most frequently sighted near the mainland, where they're thought to feed mainly on juvenile harbor seals. In fall and winter, white sharks turn up off the Farallones, where they're known to attack juvenile elephant seals and sea lions. Researchers suspect these sharks move into a favorable eating area and stay as long as the feeding is good, then depart until the following year.

White shark attacks seem to occur in greater numbers near seal and sea lion colonies off the Farallones.

According to catch records, different-sized white sharks appear to live at different places along the California coast. Young sharks are almost exclusively caught south of Pt. Conception, while adults are more commonly caught to the north. Females, too, are more frequently captured in southern California, while males show the opposite pattern. Some scientists think female white sharks give birth to their young in southern or Baja California, then return to northern California to feed. Young white sharks may also travel north as they age.

Over the years, the number of white shark sightings off northern California, and especially the Farallones, has been rising. One theory holds that the white shark population in central California is increasing because of the dramatic rise in the number of seals and sea lions—partly a result of the Marine Mammal Protection Act of 1972. According to this theory, more seals and sea lions mean more white sharks in the area and, therefore, the possibility of more attacks on people.

However, since white sharks mature slowly and breed late in life, it may be another 15 to 20 years before scientists can fully

White sharks are the largest predatory sharks in the ocean, and may reach lengths of more than 20 feet.

test this theory. In addition, the increase in the number of sightings of white shark has yet to coincide with an increase in the frequency of attacks—even though more and more people swim, surf and dive in those waters every year. This finding leads many scientists to believe that the white shark population may not be increasing at all.

Commercial fishermen catch over a dozen white sharks off California every year, but most are small, around 8 to 10 feet long. Even this small catch could reverse any supposed increase in the shark's numbers. For instance, during the summer of 1982, when fishermen netted four white sharks each over 10 feet long off the Farallones, the number of white shark sightings in that area plummeted.

Most of what we've learned about the white shark centers on its eating habits. The largest predatory fish on earth, the white shark will eat almost anything it can sink its teeth into, including fishes, birds, whales, seals, dolphins and sea turtles. White sharks are also scavengers and sometimes feed on dead or dying whales. In Monterey Bay and other parts of central California, white sharks occasionally attack sea otters, although no one knows for sure if the sharks actually end up eating them. Some scientists think white sharks may mistake sea otters for seals. Unfortunately for the otters, mistakes of this kind are usually fatal, even if the shark doesn't eat its victims.

A white shark's diet depends largely on its size. Small white sharks feed mainly on small prey and have long pointed teeth, useful for grasping slippery fishes. Large sharks, on the other hand, have broad, sharply serrated, triangular teeth, more suited to tearing apart seals and sea lions. No one's quite sure how often white sharks feed, but they're thought to gorge themselves, then fast for several days, weeks or even months.

Scientists think white sharks use a variety of senses to home in on their prey. Over distances of more than 50 feet, the sharks probably rely on their hearing or sense of smell. Over shorter

Elephant seals and other marine mammals, abundant along parts of the California coast, seem to be a staple of a white shark's diet.

distances, they seem to depend more on sight. At extremely close range, they may even zero in on the weak electrical signals produced by their prey.

Once it senses food in the water, a hungry white shark often moves in quickly from below, catching its prey off guard. As it swims toward its victim, the shark lifts its snout, dislocates its jaws and takes a huge bite—all within less than a second. With such stealth and power, it's easy to see why the white shark is considered one of the supreme predators of the sea.

A white shark doesn't always devour its prey on the first bite. After making an initial attack, the shark usually backs off and swims cautiously around its prey—presumably to wait for its victim to bleed to death or lapse into shock. Within minutes, the shark returns to finish off the job, although sometimes it swims away. Dr. John McCosker, director of the Steinhart Aquarium in San Francisco, calls this the "bite-and-spit" strategy. According to McCosker, the white shark's unusual feeding behavior may prevent the shark from being injured by a flailing seal or sea lion. This wait-and-see attitude has been directly responsible for the survival of many human victims, who were able to leave the water before the shark returned.

White sharks are extremely difficult to keep in captivity. Only a few have been captured alive and none has survived very long. In 1981, researchers at Sea World in San Diego kept a white shark alive for 16 days. In 1984, the Monterey Bay Aquarium received a four-foot, ten-inch white shark that was netted in the waters off Bodega Bay, just north of San Francisco. Aquarium staff drove to Bodega Bay Marine Laboratory, where the 100-pound male had been kept in a round holding tank overnight. After loading the shark into a holding tank outfitted with oxygen and running sea water and driving to the aquarium, staff members hoisted the shark's tank into the aquarium's holding area using a large crane. The shark was then released into the aquarium's Monterey Bay Habitats exhibit.

At first, the shark bumped into the exhibit's walls, scraping its nose and pectoral fins until it learned to negotiate the turns. However, the biggest hurdle wasn't in getting the shark to swim straight, but in getting it to eat. The aquarium's husbandry staff tried everything. When they dumped buckets full of shrimp, mackerel and blood into the tank, the other sharks and fishes feasted, but the white shark wouldn't eat a bite. They even tried tying live fish onto poles and dragging them through the water in hopes of enticing the shark to feed. But nothing happened. Finally, divers swam next to the shark and attempted to feed it by hand. Still the shark wouldn't eat. After eleven days without food, the white shark died.

In the future, the aquarium's husbandry staff plan to use other techniques to maintain a white shark on exhibit. Increasing the water temperature in the shark's tank and administering feeding stimulants could help to increase the shark's appetite and improve its chances of survival.

A 100-pound male white shark lived in an exhibit at the Monterey Bay Aquarium for eleven days. To date, no one's been able to keep a white shark alive in an aquarium for long.

Shortfin makos, left, roam the open seas, feeding on fast-swimming fishes like this school of jack-mackerel, above.

While not as large as the white shark, the shortfin mako, also known as the bonito shark, is another formidable predator found in Monterey Bay. Strong and agile swimmers, makos are designed for distance and speed. Their bodies are built like torpedoes with fins, the same energy-efficient shape as mackerel and tuna. The mako also has smoother skin than most other sharks. Its flattened denticles have ridges that channel water smoothly over the shark's body, which reduces drag in the water and increases speed.

Along with sleek, streamlined bodies, makos have powerful tail fins equipped with a built-in keel—a flattened portion that gives the shark extra thrust and helps stabilize it at high speeds. Makos can swim about 30 miles per hour over short distances—faster than many motor boats.

Heat from the high-speed mako's bloodstream is retained inside its body, rather than dissipated through its gills or at the surface of its skin, as in most other sharks. By retaining this heat, makos can elevate their body temperatures above the temperature of the surrounding water. This increase in body temperature speeds up contractions of the shark's muscles and contributes to the shark's tremendous speed and strength.

Makos feed primarily on fast-swimming fishes, including mackerel and bonito. Occasionally, these sharks will race through dense schools with their mouths wide open, snapping up fishes right and left. Makos have also been known to go after much larger prey, including swordfish. In one case, a 720-pound mako caught off Bimini in the Bahamas had a 110-pound swordfish in its stomach, completely intact except for the tail. To maintain its high metabolism, a mako needs to eat large quantities of food. Studies of food habits conducted off the East Coast found that a typical 140-pound mako might eat as much as 15 times its body weight in a single year.

Because of the mako's speed and strength, sport fishermen consider it one of the premier saltwater game fishes. A hooked mako will fight hard and long, sometimes leaping out of the water in an effort to shake itself free. Hooked makos have even been known to charge boats, sometimes jumping right onto the deck— much to the surprise of the fishermen onboard! People who have eaten mako say it's one of the best-tasting of all sharks. Makos are sometimes seen in the Monterey Bay during summer and fall, running with schooling fishes.

Most of the open-ocean sharks that live in Monterey Bay are seasonal visitors. Blue sharks, for instance, commonly show up for a few months in late summer and early fall. The majority of these are immature females. The rest of the population appears to remain off southern California and northern Mexico.

No one's quite certain why blue sharks split up this way, although a similar pattern has been found along the East Coast, where female blues are typically found much farther north than males. Juveniles may spread far and wide, while adults may stick closer to breeding areas. When males and females do come together, their encounters may turn violent. Adult females often bear

This blue shark, accompanied by a pilot-fish in warmer waters farther south, is a citizen of the open sea. Young female blues venture north into the bay during the summer and fall.

deep scars along their backs and fins, possibly stemming from bites by males during courtship and mating. Fortunately, female blue sharks have thick skins; their hides are nearly three times as thick as those of males. This extra padding may help protect females during seasonal courtship encounters.

Most female blues don't mate until they're at least four or five years old. Even then, a female that mates for the first time may have yet to produce viable eggs. She'll store the male's sperm in her body for nearly a year while her eggs develop. Once she becomes sexually mature, a female blue may give birth to as many as 135 pups in a single litter.

Blue sharks are one of the most abundant sharks in the world. Yet local fishermen rarely fish for them, mainly because the blue shark's flesh contains high levels of urea and other waste products that can spoil its flavor if the shark isn't processed quickly.

Instead, the thresher shark is the most sought-after shark in the Pacific Ocean off California, including Monterey Bay. In the mid-1980s, the local fishery for these sharks flourished. The succulent white meat of the thresher is so light and tender that seafood novices often mistake it for swordfish.

But there's no mistaking a thresher in the water. You can easily distinguish this shark by its long tail, which may be nearly half the length of the shark's body. Its unusual tail has earned the thresher a host of colorful nicknames, including the "foxtail," "swingletail" and "sickletail" shark.

A thresher shark's tail propels it rapidly through schools of fast-swimming fish; it also aids in the hunt. To capture fish, the thresher whips its tail like a deadly flail, stunning or killing its prey at the surface, then swallowing it whole. A thresher will even thrash its tail at a baited hook, which explains why fishermen sometimes hook a thresher by its tail instead of its mouth.

Recent studies suggest the thresher shark population along the California coast may be declining. Between 1982 and 1987, the number of threshers caught off California increased, then both numbers and average size dropped dramatically—down several hundred thousand pounds a year. Part of this decline resulted

Thresher shark

from new restrictions placed on the fishery. Since 1986, commercial fishermen along the California coast have been prevented from catching threshers during the prime fishing season, which limits their total catch. Some scientists and fishermen fear that the lower numbers of threshers being caught is a signal that the local population is being overfished. The California Department of Fish and Game, working with other agencies, is now developing a management plan in hopes of establishing a self-sustaining fishery in the future.

In Monterey Bay, local fishermen occasionally net soupfin sharks (*Galeorhinus zyopterus*), though not nearly as often as they used to. In summer, these open-ocean sharks move close to shore where they're sometimes trapped in gill nets. As their name suggests, soupfins are prized for their fins, which are used in a number of Oriental dishes, including such delicacies as *yu chi*, the traditional sharkfin soup.

During the 1930s and '40s, however, the soupfin shark was fished primarily for its liver, which contains oil rich in vitamin A. During World War II, soupfins were the most heavily fished sharks off California. Today, they represent only a small percentage of the overall shark catch. Overfishing greatly reduced their abundance.

Like the soupfin, the largest shark in Monterey Bay also lives in the open sea. The 45-foot basking shark (*Cetorhinus maximus*) is one of the world's largest fishes—second only to the whale shark. These giant sharks can grow to be as long as a bus and weigh over six tons.

You'll most often see basking sharks off central California in fall and winter. Novices may mistake these mild-mannered sharks for white sharks because of their huge size, grayish skin and large triangular dorsal fins, among other similarities.

Unlike white sharks, though, basking sharks are harmless. Basking shark teeth are no bigger than the fingernail on your little finger. To feed, a basking shark cruises through surface waters with its mouth wide open, straining thousands of gallons of water.

Photos of feeding basking sharks are almost always murky, since they feed on tiny plankton that cloud the water with their sheer numbers.

Plankton and small fishes become trapped on the shark's comb-like gill rakers. These enormous filters line the inside of the shark's gill slits and are coated with a sticky mucus that helps trap food. When its gill rakers are full, the basking shark closes its huge mouth and swallows, sometimes taking in hundreds of pounds of plankton in a single gulp. Researchers estimate that it takes more than a half-ton of plankton to fill a large basking shark's stomach.

In Monterey Bay, an airplane pilot once spotted more than 2,000 basking sharks feeding at the surface. Smaller groups are sometimes seen swimming head to tail, moving through the water like an armada of ships. The basking shark's surface-feeding habits have made it an easy target for commercial fishermen. During the 1940s, fishermen in Monterey Bay hunted the basking shark for its flesh and huge liver. The liver of a single basking shark provided as much as 400 gallons of oil, used mainly for tanning leather. Overfishing nearly wiped out Monterey Bay populations and, though once abundant, basking sharks are now only occasionally spotted in local waters.

DEEP SEA   The largest and deepest undersea canyon along North America's west coast cuts through the very heart of Monterey Bay. This huge chasm, called the Monterey Canyon, is similar in size and shape to Arizona's Grand Canyon.

Within a few miles of shore, the bottom of the bay drops off abruptly. This gently sloping plain plunges thousands of feet to the ocean floor, forming a deep, V-shaped gorge. From its beginnings off Moss Landing, the canyon stretches nearly 60 miles out to sea, descending from a depth of 60 feet to more than two miles at its seaward edge, where it merges with the deep ocean floor. The canyon's nearshore depths draw deep-sea sharks unusually close to land.

As you descend into this vast undersea canyon, sunlight from the surface fades quickly to a dim twilight and then darkness. The water grows bitterly cold—close to freezing—and the pressure from the surrounding water becomes intense. At 3,000 feet—the depth of the canyon as it leaves the bay—the pressure per square inch is 100 times greater than at the surface.

Because the canyon is so harsh and remote, we know very little about the sharks that live there. Occasionally, commercial fishermen in the bay net deep-sea sharks while trawling for sole and rockfishes or trapping sablefish. Sport fishermen, too, sometimes hook deep-sea sharks off Moss Landing, where the canyon lies closest to shore.

In recent years, scientists have begun studying the canyon's sharks using manned submersibles and other vehicles. In 1985, scientists from the Monterey Bay Aquarium Research Institute (MBARI) and other institutions completed several canyon dives aboard the submersible *Deep Rover*. During one of their dives, the scientists photographed and collected two filetail cat sharks as they cruised past the sub's observation windows.

The Monterey Canyon cuts through Monterey Bay, and brings many deep-sea denizens close to shore.

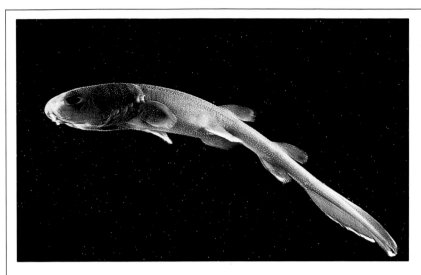

This six-inch-long juvenile deep-sea filetail cat shark will only reach a length of two feet as an adult.

Since then, the canyon has served as the focal point of numerous deep-sea expeditions. In 1988, a scientist and a photographer from the National Geographic Society completed a series of deep dives aboard the submersible *Alvin*. While diving more than a mile-and-a-half down, the crew observed and photographed a Pacific sleeper shark swimming around a baited trap they'd set in the canyon.

Currently, MBARI scientists are continuing to explore the canyon's depths using a remotely operated vehicle (ROV) named *Ventana*, meaning "window." Equipped with a video camera, the ROV transmits images from depths of nearly 1,200 feet, and researchers plan to send it even deeper in the near future. Scientists hope their state-of-the-art ROV will lead to further and deeper observations of the canyon's inhabitants, including sharks.

For now, though, deep-sea sharks, particularly in the bay, remain largely a mystery. Scientists have yet to discover even the most basic facts about these animals' lives, such as when they breed or how long they live. We do know these sharks share certain characteristics that set them apart from their surface-dwelling counterparts. Over time, their bodies and habits have adapted to the harsh conditions of the deep sea that include pressure, scarce food, no light and very cold temperatures.

While the enormous pressure in the canyon prevents many fishes from living there, it poses few problems for sharks. Some species, like the spiny dogfish, move freely between canyon depths and the surface. Others, like the filetail cat shark, begin life as eggs laid in clusters on certain spots on the bottom, spend early life in a region called the midwater zone, then return to deeper water as they get older.

Unlike most fishes, sharks are little affected by water pressure because they lack the gas-filled swimbladder found in most bony fishes. The gases in a bony fish's swimbladder—used to regulate its buoyancy—expand rapidly when a fish caught in deep water is pulled to the surface too quickly. The swimbladder expands and may eventually burst, damaging the fish's internal organs. The liquid-filled tissues of a shark, however, rarely expand, regardless of depth. One exception may be the brown cat shark (*Apristurus brunneus*), which always seems to come up floating.

The deepest parts of the ocean are perpetually dark, and without adequate sunlight, plants can't grow. The absence of plants, in turn, limits the number of animals, and food in the deep sea is scarce. To survive, deep-sea sharks make the most out of every meal. They'll eat almost anything that crosses their path, including fishes, octopuses, squid and crustaceans. Some sharks also feed on leftovers from the surface, including dead and dying animals that drift down from above.

Not all deep-sea sharks rely on this meager menu. Faced with a shortage of food, the sixgill shark may actually migrate to the surface to feed at night, retreating to deep water during the day. Although the details of their movements are little understood, sixgills are known to make rapid ascents. These sharks have been seen swimming from deep water straight up to the surface while pursuing deep-sea sharks pulled up by fishermen.

Most sunlight that reaches the ocean is reflected or absorbed near the surface; only a glimmer ever reaches the midwater zone, while the deep sea remains in darkness. To compensate for the lack of light, many sharks that live in the midwater zone have well-developed eyes that contain large numbers of light-perceiving cells, or "rods." This modification is also seen among nocturnal animals on land which, like deep-sea sharks, rarely see the light of day.

Sharks also make use of a reflecting layer of cells behind their eyes called the *tapetum lucidum* (ta-**pee**-tum loo-**see**-dum). Cats also have a tapetum behind each eye, which allows them to see at night when they hunt. Most of us have seen the effect when our car headlights catch the eyes of a cat at night. The tapetum acts like a mirror, reflecting light back onto the eye once it has passed through the retina—in effect, doubling the amount of light available to the animal, whether shark or cat. This catlike feature earned cat sharks their name; their slanty eyes glow an eerie green when exposed to light. People don't have tapeta. The backs of our eyes are black and absorb light after it passes through the retinas.

Surface-dwelling sharks darken and protect their tapeta in bright sunlight with a layer of movable pigment, but a cat shark's tapeta are always exposed. Cat sharks, unlike other sharks, can change the size of their pupils—the opening in the eye where light shines through. By adjusting the shape of their pupils from a narrow slit to a large circle, cat sharks control the amount of light reaching their eyes.

Not all deep-dwelling sharks have such well-developed eyes. Unlike sharks that live in the midwater zone, sharks that live along the deep ocean floor tend to have poor eyesight and must rely on their other senses. These sharks may only see brief flashes of bioluminescent light and have no need for such sensitive eyes.

Deep-sea sharks have adapted to the harsh conditions of their environment, resulting in vastly different body types and lifestyles

compared to surface-dwelling sharks. Surface sharks, for instance, are generally active predators with strong, muscular bodies and rigid skeletons. Deep-sea sharks, on the other hand, are generally slow swimmers with limp body tissues and weak skeletons. Why the difference? While surface sharks can eat enough to support their muscular bodies and active lifestyles, deep-sea sharks must pare down their bodies and conserve limited food reserves. The freezing water and intense pressure lowers their metabolic rates, leaving many deep-sea sharks slow-moving and lethargic.

The sleeper shark is a perfect example of a deep-sea shark. As its name implies, it's extremely sluggish, soft and flabby, not sleek and streamlined like most open-ocean sharks. Unlike those sharks, a sleeper shark wastes little energy trying to stay afloat. Low muscle mass and a lightweight skeleton help the shark maintain its buoyancy in the water. The sleeper shark probably spends most of its time cruising slowly above the bottom, waiting for fishes or other prey to swim within easy reach.

Deep-sea sharks differ from open-ocean sharks in other ways. Sharks that race through surface waters have almost-smooth denticles that reduce drag, thus increasing speed. But deep-sea sharks tend to have sharp, bumpy denticles that increase drag and slow them down. The skin of the prickly shark (*Echinorhinus cookei*), for instance, is studded with clusters of sharp, thornlike denticles that can cut and scrape your hand if you handle the shark the wrong way. While this armor may slow it down, it may also help shield the prickly shark from predators, including other deep-sea sharks.

The Monterey Bay Aquarium Research Institute's scientists seek new glimpses of deep-sea sharks and other sea life using this remotely operated vehicle outfitted with video cameras and collecting gear.

SHARK ATTACKS

Sharks are often portrayed as ferocious predators of helpless swimmers. Yet while millions of sharks roam the sea, an average of fewer than 30 to 50 people each year is reportedly attacked by sharks worldwide, and only about a third of these encounters prove fatal. Although scientists have yet to fully understand why sharks attack people, one thing is clear: the odds of being bitten by a shark are extremely low.

Since the 1960s, biologists from the California Department of Fish and Game have been researching and documenting shark attacks off the coast of California. Their records show that from 1926 to June 1989, 63 people were attacked by sharks; eight of these encounters were fatal. Although biologists admit that some attacks may have gone unreported, their statistics show a yearly average of only one attack along the entire California coast.

One of the earliest known attacks off California took place in Monterey Bay in 1881. Although the event was never included in official records, details of the attack appeared in two local newspapers. Both newspapers reported that on June 25, 1881, Father Thomas Hudson, a Catholic priest from the nearby town of Gilroy, was swimming off Santa Cruz when he was attacked by a large shark.

Although Hudson managed to escape, he suffered severe wounds, including a deep gash along his right thigh and a torn left heel. According to the *Santa Cruz Courier and Local Item*, the attack "created great surprise and aroused many fears with the more timid, as it was the first instance ever known of a fighting fish in these waters."

The following day, fishermen netted a shark in the bay, which the newspapers variously described as a "thrasher" and a "dog-fish." Although both papers claimed the shark caught was the one that had attacked Hudson, scientists today doubt the authenticity of these early reports, especially since thresher sharks and dogfish have never been implicated in attacks.

Nevertheless, the *Courier* reported that the shark's capture helped calm the fears of local residents. According to the paper, "Confidence in the safety of the bathing grounds was speedily restored, as the visit of such a fish to this Bay [sic] is rarer than the appearance of a comet in the heavens."

In 1952, Monterey Bay gained notoriety once again when it became the site of the first fatal shark attack off California. On December 7, 17-year-old Barry Wilson was mauled by a white shark while swimming off Lovers Point in Monterey. A friend of Wilson's, as well as four other divers who were in the water at the time, immediately swam to Wilson's aid.

However, by the time they got the teenager to shore, Wilson was already dead. According to reports in the *Monterey Peninsula Herald*, hundreds of onlookers soon gathered on the beach and news of the attack spread quickly. Within days, newspapers across the country were printing front-page stories about Wilson's tragic death. Since then, there have been several other shark attacks in and around Monterey Bay. However, none has received more national attention than the attack on Lewis Boren in 1981.

On December 19, 24-year-old Boren was surfing alone off Pebble Beach when he reportedly disappeared. The next day, Boren's blood-stained surfboard washed up on shore with a large crescent-shaped bite taken out of the side. Biologists from the Fish and Game Department identified teeth markings on the board as those of a white shark estimated to be 17 to 19 feet long—the largest ever reported for the area.

Boren's disappearance and the discovery of his surfboard generated newspaper headlines and television news stories across the nation. Five days after the attack, Boren's body washed up on shore. Hordes of reporters and curious onlookers descended on Monterey. Despite an intensive and well-publicized search, the shark that attacked Boren was never found.

One theory suggests that white shark attacks are really cases of mistaken identity. Compare this shark's-eye-view of a diving sea lion to the profiles of a surfer and snorkeler.

Today, experts say the greatest risk of attack in Monterey Bay continues to stem from white sharks, which, though rare, are sometimes spotted in local waters. Since all white shark attacks in California have occurred outside kelp forests, researchers advise swimmers to stick near kelp and to avoid areas that support large colonies of seals and sea lions, the white shark's primary prey. In addition, scuba divers should spend as little time as possible near the water's surface, where the majority of attacks in California have taken place. One theory proposed by Dr. John McCosker of the Steinhart Aquarium points out the resemblance of a wet-suited surfer on a surfboard to that of a sea lion at the surface, suggesting that shark attacks may be cases of mistaken identity. Most researchers agree that sharks do not seem to be seeking out human prey.

FISHING FOR SHARKS

For centuries, we've hunted sharks. Among the first to seek sharks in Monterey Bay were the Ohlone Indians, who lived in scattered villages throughout California's central coast. Animal remains excavated from a village site near Elkhorn Slough suggest the resident Ohlones feasted heavily on bat rays and leopard sharks as far back as 2,000 years ago.

Chinese immigrants arriving in the Monterey Bay area in the mid-1800s were the first to establish a commercial shark fishery in the region. The sharks were fished primarily for their fins, which were dried and exported to fish markets in San Francisco and China.

During those years, Portuguese whalers sometimes hunted basking sharks in the bay, mainly for sport and practice. Rowing their boats alongside the docile sharks, the whalers speared them with iron harpoons used to hunt whales. The sharks were slaughtered for their giant livers, which were boiled in large pots to extract their oil. The oil was later made into soap or burned in oil lamps.

During the 1920s, party-boat operators in the bay began a small sport fishery for basking sharks. Like the Portuguese whalers before them, the fishermen used whale harpoons to capture the huge sharks, driving the harpoons by hand. The sharks were eventually processed into dog biscuits and commercial livestock feeds and, in the case of the liver oil, sold as a health tonic.

In 1937, a major shark fishery developed in the bay. That year, scientists discovered that liver oil from the soupfin shark contained tremendous quantities of vitamin A—nearly 100 times that of cod-liver oil. Until World War II, cod-liver oil had been the primary source of vitamin A in Europe and the United States. Once the war broke out, German submarines cut off the supply of cod from the North Atlantic, and the demand for shark liver oil skyrocketed.

Along the Pacific coast, hundreds of fishermen began collecting the prized soupfin,

These shark fishermen, top, have already sliced the fins off the sharks piled in the bottom of their lampara boat, photographed near Capitola in the early 1900s.

Above, sharks litter the beach of a Chinese fishing village near Monterey, around 1890.

setting off what many observers described as a fishing boom akin to the Gold Rush of the 1850s. The fabulous prices offered for the sharks attracted people from all walks of life, and according to one biologist, "almost anything that would float was used for shark fishing."

Much of the shark oil produced during those years was sold to the United States government and processed into vitamin capsules. Military officials hoped the vitamin A in the oil would improve the night vision of Allied pilots fighting overseas. Back at home, farmers relied on the oil to increase livestock production so they could feed a hungry nation at war.

The tremendous boom in the bay's shark fishery proved to be short-lived. By 1944, just seven years after the fishery's start, shark landings in Monterey Bay had plummeted. Scientists later attributed this rapid decline to overfishing. The fishery suffered another setback in 1949, when researchers discovered a way to produce vitamin A synthetically. That discovery, combined with the declining numbers of sharks, virtually shut down the soupfin fishery.

The bay's basking shark fishery followed a similar decline. In 1946, owners of the Hovden Food Products Corporation in Moss Landing encouraged some of the local fishermen to hunt for basking sharks. The shark's liver contained hundreds of gallons of oil which, though low in vitamin A, could be used for making paint and soap or tanning leather.

As in previous years, fishermen hunted the sharks with large harpoons. In 1947, fishermen began hiring pilots to fly over the bay and locate sharks swimming below the ocean's surface. The use of spotter planes greatly increased the fishermen's catch, and by 1950, few basking sharks were left. By then, the demand for shark oil had fallen off, making it uneconomical to hunt the few remaining sharks.

During the following years, the shark fishery in Monterey Bay languished as fishermen turned to more valuable catches, such as halibut, rockfishes, salmon, sole, sanddabs and squid. However, an increasing demand for fresh shark meat in recent years has spurred another boom in the local shark fishery. Today, leopard, thresher, shortfin mako and soupfin sharks are caught in the bay and sold in fish markets throughout the state. A small market for shark fins also exists.

In addition to these commercial ventures, the shark population also supports a sizeable sportfishing industry. Since the early 1950s, shark derbies held at Elkhorn Slough have become an annual event, pulling in hundreds of fishermen from throughout central California. Interestingly, the largest "shark" caught in the derby as of 1989 was a female bat ray!

To prevent the slough from being overfished, scientists from Moss Landing Marine Laboratories, Monterey Bay Aquarium and the Elkhorn Slough National Estuarine Research Reserve, plus Elkhorn Slough Foundation volunteers have been encouraging derby fishermen to throw back sharks and rays that fail to meet a certain size limit, and have been helping them weigh their catch before tagging and releasing larger ones. They're hoping to maintain the health of the shark fishery while at the same time learn more about shark populations, age, growth and movement.

During the Elkhorn Slough Shark Derby, biologists weigh, tag and release sharks and rays.

4

SHARKS AND RAYS ON EXHIBIT

Until the 1970s, most aquarium sharks were housed in circular tanks or pools. Although these conventional tanks proved adequate for small sharks, large sharks often grew sick and died. Research later showed that large sharks kept in circular tanks expend vast amounts of energy navigating the curves and are much like runners who never have a chance to sit down. Scientists theorized that a constantly turning shark might build up dangerous levels of lactic acid and other metabolic wastes in its tissues—a condition which, if prolonged, could ultimately prove fatal.

To avoid this problem, Monterey Bay Aquarium planners, supervised by director of husbandry David Powell, decided on a radically different design for their large Monterey Bay Habitats exhibit so that it could safely accommodate large sharks, including sevengills. The 325,000-gallon exhibit is shaped like a giant hourglass, with wide turnarounds at each end. The tank's 90-foot straightaway gives the sharks a long glide path for resting and breathing, and has prevented the problems of stress seen in many other captive sharks.

The aquarium's planners also avoided placing water filters, pumps or other metal equipment inside or near the new exhibit. Past studies revealed that weak electrical currents generated by these parts could cause sharks to become disoriented and swim into the sides of their tank. Even the steel reinforcing bars inside the concrete walls received a coating of epoxy to prevent corrosion from sea water and to reduce the intensity of electrical fields emanating from the steel.

Planning for all of the aquarium's shark-related exhibits began in early 1980, nearly four years before the aquarium's opening. Unlike most public aquariums, which showcase their specimens apart from their natural neighbors, the Monterey Bay Aquarium displays local varieties of sharks and rays side by side with fishes and invertebrates in lifelike habitat exhibits simulating conditions in the wild.

Despite the years of planning, the aquarium's husbandry staff encountered some unexpected problems. For instance, when the sharks were introduced to the Monterey Bay Habitats exhibit, a curious thing happened. During the day, the sharks maneuvered through their tank with ease. But at night, they became clumsy and occasionally collided with the walls. Staff members soon realized the animals were having trouble seeing in the dark. To solve the problem, they installed small fluorescent night lights above the exhibit. The trick worked so well that now all the aquarium's main exhibits have night lights.

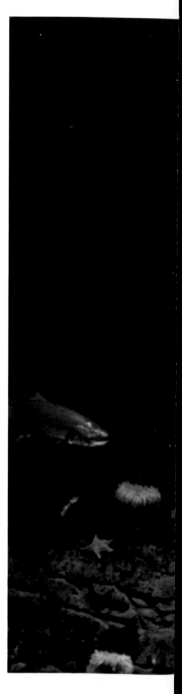

The Monterey Bay Habitats exhibit at the Monterey Bay Aquarium showcases large sharks and rays along with other local residents.

Large sharks arrive at the aquarium in oval transport tanks, left, and are hoisted by crane to the second-floor exhibit area.

COLLECTING SHARKS Where do aquariums get their sharks? Some are caught by local fishermen. The majority, however, are collected by aquarium staff and, in the case of the Monterey Bay Aquarium, from sites in and around Monterey Bay.

Occasionally, the aquarium's collecting team travels farther afield. Just prior to opening, staff members organized an expedition to the Channel Islands off southern California to collect warm-water fishes, including swell sharks and horn sharks, both rare in Monterey Bay. Working mostly at night, scuba divers searched for the sharks among rocks at the base of the kelp forest. Divers coaxed the sharks into large nylon-mesh bags, then transferred them into holding tanks at the surface.

Capturing the aquarium's sevengill shark proved to be one of the team's greatest collecting challenges. Like many sharks, sevengills are extremely delicate and easily injured when pulled from the water. For years, aquariums across the country have had only limited success in keeping sevengills alive, often because the animals were badly injured during capture and transport.

To collect the aquarium's sevengill, husbandry staff traveled to Humboldt Bay in northern California, where the sharks congregate during spring and summer. After several days of fishing, the collecting team hooked a six-foot-long male. They quickly positioned the struggling shark alongside the boat, then eased it onto a canvas stretcher. Once the 100-pound shark was secured, they hoisted it into an eight-foot holding tank outfitted with an oxygen tank and a small pump for circulating sea water. The super-oxygenated water in the tank helped increase the flow of oxygen over the shark's gills. The oxygen also had a tranquilizing effect, keeping the shark calm during transport and handling.

Back at the pier, the sevengill was again loaded onto the stretcher and lifted into a large oval transport tank equipped with

oxygen and pump. From there, a pickup truck transported the shark some 400 miles to the aquarium. During the 10-hour drive, the team periodically checked on the shark to make sure the animal was healthy and breathing normally.

Most newly captured sharks that arrive at the aquarium spend their first week or two in a special quarantine area, where staff members treat them for external parasites or diseases that might infect other fishes. But the sevengill shark was too delicate and too large to handle the extra stop. Using a giant crane, husbandry staff hoisted the shark's transport tank into the aquarium's exhibit area and released the shark directly into his new home.

At first, the sevengill seemed disoriented and occasionally collided with the sides of the exhibit. After several hours, though, he was swimming normally and within a couple of weeks was eating on his own. Since then, the first young male—christened Blackie by the aquarium's husbandry staff—has been joined by five other sevengills, all juveniles donated by the Steinhart Aquarium in San Francisco.

Although sevengill sharks have been known to feast on their tankmates, aquarium fishes have been lucky so far. Despite his large size and imposing teeth, Blackie has never attacked the other fishes on display and shows no signs of aggression. Aquarium staff suspect the cool water in the tank keeps the shark somewhat docile. A balanced diet may also explain Blackie's apparent disinterest in the other fishes.

Visitors delight in watching sharks swim just inches from their noses, and wonder why the large predators don't eat the other fishes. (We keep them all well-fed.)

CARE AND FEEDING Regardless of how natural they appear, shark displays in an aquarium operate differently from natural communities in the sea. Aquarium staff must intervene in processes like feeding and health care to create exhibits that are both pleasing to look at and useful for teaching and research. The behind-the-scenes stories are as intriguing as the exhibits themselves.

Sharks and rays receive special diets depending on their individual needs. Most small sharks, like the leopard sharks and smoothhounds, are fed twice a day along with the other fishes. Aquarists stand on platforms above the exhibits and throw food into the water. Because no one knows exactly what kind of nutrients sharks need to stay healthy, staff provide them with a wide variety of seafood, including krill, anchovies, squid, smelt, salmon and mackerel.

Sharks like the sevengills require a different diet and feeding schedule. Because sevengills have slow metabolic rates and need relatively little food, they're fed salmon fillets enriched with multiple vitamins only once or twice a week, with an occasional herring treat thrown in. The change in diet ensures the sharks are getting the full range of nutrients they need, and keeps the fussier sharks interested in feeding.

How do you feed a hungry shark? Aquarists place food on long poles so the sharks can feed without scraping their mouths on the bottom.

At first, aquarists fed the sevengills just like the other sharks. They tossed in the fish and let the sevengills feed along the bottom. But the sharks scraped their noses raw on the exhibit's rocky bottom. Now, an aquarist clips the fish to an eight-foot-long pole and feeds each shark individually. Using the pole like a long arm, the aquarist places the fish just below the shark's nose, allowing the shark to eat as much as it wants. How much do the aquarium's sevengills eat? Not much, by human standards. Blackie, the largest of the group, eats about five to seven pounds of food a month. Each juvenile consumes from two to six pounds a month.

Like the sevengills, the bat rays in the aquarium's Bat Ray Pool also receive special attention. During twice-daily feeding sessions, an aquarist lures the rays to the side of their pool using the aquarium's version of a bat ray dinner bell—two ribbed fiberglass sticks rubbed together under water. The grating noise produced by the sticks attracts the rays' attention and within minutes the entire group is swarming at the side of the pool. After a brief lesson from the aquarist, visitors take turns hand-feeding the gentle rays, offering them a combination of shrimp, squid and clams. To protect visitors from an accidental injury, aquarists clip and remove the bat rays' stinging spines.

The bat ray exhibit, left, invites you to reach out and touch a ray swimming past in this shallow pool.

Divers in the Kelp Forest exhibit, above, hand-feed sharks and other kelp inhabitants while talking to visitors through a microphone in the mask.

AQUARIUM RESEARCH A source of education and entertainment for visitors, sharks on exhibit also serve as a resource for scientists. Since 1985, Monterey Bay Aquarium staff have been conducting several long-term research projects on captive sharks they can monitor under carefully controlled conditions. Most of the studies focus on developing new husbandry techniques or comparing captive sharks to those in the wild.

One of the longest-running projects examines the growth and feeding habits of sevengill sharks. Researchers want to identify the sharks' feeding cycles, determine what factors affect their food intake, and find out how efficiently they use their food.

During weekly feeding sessions, an aquarium volunteer identifies the sharks by external markings and records how much food each shark eats. Over time, aquarium researchers have discovered that the sevengills' food intake follows a regular cycle. If the sharks gorge themselves one week, they're much more likely to eat less in the following weeks, or skip a meal altogether. The feeding peaks occur roughly two to three weeks apart—a pattern that may correspond to feeding habits of wild sevengills.

Researchers are also finding that a sevengill's appetite fluctuates with the changing seasons. What causes this variability? One factor may be temperature. Since the aquarium pumps its sea water directly from Monterey Bay, water temperatures in the sharks' exhibits vary with the time of year. Cooler temperatures generally occur during spring and summer; warmer temperatures during fall and winter. The sevengills seem to eat less when temperatures are cooler, possibly because the cold water slows their metabolic rate, enabling them to get by with less food.

Aquarium researchers also monitor the sharks' growth by removing them from the exhibit every three months to weigh and measure them. During their first year, the aquarium's juvenile sevengills grew more than a foot and nearly tripled in weight. The adult sevengills, however, grew much more slowly. During his first four years at the aquarium, Blackie, the aquarium's largest sevengill, grew less than an inch and gained only about a pound.

Research on shark growth rates and feeding habits in aquariums, left, as well as observations of wild sharks, above, help us learn more about the lives of sharks and rays.

TAGGING SHARKS

A school of spiny dogfish darts by the window of an aquarium exhibit. How do you distinguish one dogfish from the next? For the aquarists who feed and care for these sharks, it's an important question.

Identifying individual sharks allows aquarists to record an individual's food intake and growth or monitor changes in its health. Staff at the Monterey Bay Aquarium have been experimenting with an innovative identification system that lets them keep tabs on individual sharks and rays. The heart of this system is a tiny identification tag, equipped with a microchip and encased in a glass capsule, about the size and shape of a pencil lead. Each microchip is encoded with a unique 10-digit number that distinguishes one tag from the next. Using a surgical syringe equipped with a hypodermic needle, the aquarium's veterinarian Dr. Tom Williams injects the tiny implant into the shark's back, just below the skin.

Once implanted, the tag works much like the computerized bar codes printed on packaged grocery items. After removing the tagged shark from the exhibit and placing it in a shallow holding tank, aquarists pass a computerized scanning wand along the shark's back. Like the stationary scanners built into supermarket check-out lines, the wand automatically reads the number encoded on the tag. A high-pitched "beep" from the scanner lets you know the tag has been properly read.

Public aquariums have been tagging their sharks for years. Most clip plastic tags to the shark's fin or back. However, these external tags have several built-in drawbacks. Over time, they fall off and become lost, or become difficult to read. In some cases, they can even cause physical injury to the shark. Husbandry staff at the Monterey Bay Aquarium also felt external tags would detract from the natural look of the exhibits.

Implanted tags avoid these problems and are designed to last virtually forever. So far, tags have been implanted in leopard sharks, sevengill sharks and bat rays. In the meantime, a scanner designed for use in sea water is already on the drawing board so aquarists can keep a closer eye on the aquarium's sharks and rays.

Inserting a microchip under a shark's skin can be delicate work for Dr. Tom Williams, middle, assisted by Scott Nygren, left, and Leslie Williams, right.

THE TRUTH ABOUT SHARKS   Aquarium exhibits, informative labels and in-depth research programs seek to dispel the myths and misconceptions surrounding sharks. Although facts prove otherwise, many people still think of sharks as maniacal eating machines, eager to devour anything, or anyone, in their path. Sharks continue to rank among the most universally feared of all animals.

Interest in sharks, like these blue sharks, is growing, and may lead to a better understanding of these diverse fishes.

Yet this enduring image of sharks as "man-eaters" unfairly condemns a diverse group of animals. Evidence now suggests that sharks are actually more threatened than threatening, and that it's the sharks, not us, who have the most to fear.

Each year, millions of sharks are caught and killed by commercial fishermen. In 1976, the worldwide commercial shark catch totaled nearly 350 million tons, and the pressure to fish for more sharks has been on the rise. Sport fishermen, too, take a heavy toll and, in some areas of the world, "shark barriers" strung along beaches to protect swimmers net thousands of sharks a year, including harmless ones.

If sharks were like other fishes, these losses might have little effect on their overall numbers. But since sharks grow slowly, breed late in life and generally bear few young, they're extremely sensitive to overfishing. An intensive fishery can decimate a shark population in just a few years. Shark populations that have been overfished may take years or even decades to recover, if at all.

Some shark species have been overfished nearly to extinction in certain parts of the world. Biologists and fisheries managers are trying to learn more about commercially valuable species in hopes of preventing further declines.

While the future of many shark populations remains uncertain, interest in sharks is growing. Each year, millions of visitors flock to public aquariums to view sharks on display. Sport divers seek out sharks to observe and photograph them in their natural environment. In time, perhaps, knowledge and familiarity will dispel our undue fear of sharks, transforming it into a sense of wonder and respect for these magnificent animals of the sea.

A Sampling of Sharks and Rays in Monterey Bay

We're defining Monterey Bay as including all waters between Pt. Lobos and Natural Bridges State Beach, with the line between those two points forming the bay's western boundary.

Sharks (20)
Basking shark *Cetorhinus maximus*
Blue shark *Prionace glauca*
Brown cat shark *Apristurus brunneus*
Brown smoothhound *Mustelus henlei*
Filetail cat shark *Parmaturus xaniurus*
Gray smoothhound *Mustelus californicus*
Horn shark *Heterodontus francisci**
Leopard shark *Triakis semifasciata*
Pacific angel shark *Squatina californica*
Pacific sleeper shark *Somniosus pacificus*
Prickly shark *Echinorhinus cookei*

Salmon shark *Lamna ditropis*
Sevengill shark *Notorynchus cepedianus*
Shortfin mako (bonito) *Isurus oxyrinchus*
Sixgill shark *Hexanchus griseus*
Soupfin shark *Galeorhinus zyopterus*
Spiny dogfish *Squalus acanthias*
Swell shark *Cephaloscyllium ventriosum**
Thresher shark *Alopias vulpinus*
White shark *Carcharodon carcharias*

Rays (6)
Bat ray *Myliobatis californica*
Pacific electric ray *Torpedo californica*
Pelagic stingray *Dasyatis violacea**
Round stingray *Urolophus halleri**
Shovelnose guitarfish *Rhinobatos productus*
Thornback *Platyrhinoidis triseriata*

Skates (6)
Big skate *Raja binoculata*
Black skate *Bathyraja trachura*
California skate *Raja inornata*
Longnose skate *Raja rhina*
Sandpaper skate *Bathyraja kincaidi*
Starry skate *Raja stellulata*

Ratfishes (1)
Spotted ratfish *Hydrolagus colliei*

* not common in Monterey Bay

Blue shark

Skate

INDEX